The Sinister Secrets of the Deadly Desert

A play by
Katy Forde

Illustrated by
Adam Nickel

Contents

Pearson Australia
(a division of Pearson Australia Group Pty Ltd)
707 Collins Street, Melbourne, Victoria 3008
PO Box 23360, Melbourne, Victoria 8012
www.pearson.com.au

2019 2018 2017 2016
10 9 8 7 6 5 4 3 2 1

Text by Katy Forde
Illustrations by Adam Nickel

Publishers: Sabine Bolick, Beth Zeme
Project Managers: Diane Leyman, Michelle Thomas
Lead Editor: Steve Dobney
Editor: Sally Green
Proofreader: Thalia Kalkipsakis
Designer: Lisa Howard
Senior File & Asset Coordinator: Rob Curulli
Cover art: Adam Nickel
Printed by SOS Print + Media Group

ISBN 978 1 4886 1313 5

Pearson Australia Group Pty Ltd
ABN 40 004 245 943

Characters

Max

Max Lonesome
(detective)

Nancy

Nancy Green
(eco-hotel owner)

Big Bux

Hughie "Big Bux" McGee
(landowner)

Violet

Violet Highnote
(singer)

Jimmy

Jimmy Presto
(journalist)

Cindy

Cindy Sharp
(maid)

Act 1: At the New Eco-hotel

The hot desert sun is beating down. Max has just arrived at the hotel.

Max: *(to audience)* I only just got here, but already I don't like the place. Everything is too bright, too hot. A man like me belongs in the city, among the shadows and alleyways. Why did I agree to this job?

Nancy comes outside to greet Max.

Nancy: Are you the detective?

Max: Max Lonesome. You're the kid who rang me?

Nancy: Yes, I'm Nancy Green. Thank you so much for coming. Something terrible has happened!

Max: *(to audience)* This kid is in trouble, and I like trouble.

(to Nancy) What's the lowdown?

Nancy: The singing frogs have been stolen!

Max: **Singing** frogs?

Nancy: Yes! A few months ago, I opened this eco-hotel. It's beautiful here, but very remote. I needed to find something extra to attract people. That's when I heard the frogs down at the lake.

Max: And these frogs – they sang?

Nancy: Well, sort of. They made the most gorgeous sound, like water over pebbles. I called them "singing frogs". I thought they'd be the perfect way to promote my hotel, so I put ads in the newspapers: "Come and hear the singing frogs!" And, finally, lots of people started booking rooms.

Max: And then someone stole the frogs?

Nancy: Well, they must have, because suddenly the frogs **vanished**.

Max: No trace of them, huh?

Nancy: None!

Max: I'm guessing that wasn't good for business.

Nancy: Once the news got out, everyone cancelled. Now no one wants to stay at my deadly Desert Eco-hotel!

Max: **Deadly**?

Nancy: Around here, "deadly" means "amazing". And the hotel **is** amazing. But if I can't find the singing frogs, I'll have to close down!

Max: Okay, kid, take me to the lake. I need to see the scene of the crime.

Nancy leads Max to a dried-up lake.

Max: Uh – where's the lake?

Nancy: This is a claypan. It hasn't rained for a while, and the claypan only becomes a lake when it rains.

Max: *(to audience)* I knew at once what had happened. Frogs need water. How was I going to break it to Nancy that her singing frogs were dead?

(*to Nancy*) Right. Well, let's head back up to the hotel for now.

Max and Nancy arrive at the front of the hotel just as Big Bux arrives by car.

Nancy: Afternoon, Big Bux!

Big Bux: G'day, Nancy.

Nancy: Max, this is Hughie "Big Bux" McGee. He owns most of the land around here – except for mine.

Cindy comes out of the hotel.

Cindy: Ms Green! There's a phone call for you!

Big Bux: Go and answer it, Nancy. I'll show Max around.

Nancy and Cindy go inside.

Big Bux: So you're the detective she hired?

Max: What's it to you?

Big Bux: Well, I don't think the frogs were stolen.

Max: Neither do I. I think we both know what **really** happened.

Big Bux: W-we do?

Max: The lake dried up and they died.

Big Bux: Ha! You city people make me laugh. You don't understand the first thing about desert animals.

Max: Why don't you fill me in, then?

Big Bux and Max walk to the claypan.

Big Bux: Desert animals don't need much water. And they know how to find water when they need it. Take that thorny devil, for instance. It's enjoying a refreshing drink.

Max: Are you crazy? It's just standing there.

Big Bux: It's drinking with its feet. The water from the damp sand travels through the scales on its feet and up into its mouth.

Max: All right, all right, I get your drift. Desert animals can survive even if there isn't much water. So, if the frogs aren't dead or stolen, where are they?

Big Bux: They never existed.

Max: Huh?

Big Bux: Nancy's from the city. She doesn't know the desert. I reckon she heard cicadas. There's no such thing as a trilling frog.

Max: What did you say?

Big Bux: I said there's no such thing as a singing frog.

Max: You said "trilling" frog.

Big Bux: Gee, is that the time? I'd better go. It'll be dark soon.

Big Bux and Max walk back to the hotel. Big Bux drives off and Violet comes out of the hotel.

Violet: La, la, LA! Oh, hello. I didn't realise anyone was here. I'm just warming up my voice for my show tonight.

Max: You sing at the hotel?

Violet: Yes. Isn't it wonderful? I convinced Nancy to hire me as a replacement for the frogs. I dress up in a frog costume and sing for the guests. I call myself "The Fabulous Froggy".

Max: That sounds a bit strange.

Violet: Maybe, but you've got to understand: I'd do anything to sing.

Max: Anything?

Violet: **Anything!**

Jimmy comes out of the hotel and sits down.

Jimmy: Violet? Where's your costume? You don't want to disappoint your fans!

Violet: *(giggling)* What fans, Jimmy? Tonight I'll be singing for four people: you, Max, Nancy and Cindy!

Jimmy: With your talent, people will soon be lining up to hear you sing.

Violet: You're sweet, Jimmy. I think **you're** my biggest fan for now.

Violet goes back inside.

Jimmy: So, you're the detective Nancy told me about. I'm Jimmy Presto, journalist. Got any leads on the missing frogs?

Max: I'll ask the questions around here. What's a journalist doing in the desert?

Jimmy: I'm writing about the hotel for my newspaper. Lucky for me, when I got here, the frogs disappeared and Violet arrived.

Max: What do you mean, "lucky for you"?

Jimmy: I want to cover **big** stories – and now I am!

Jimmy goes back inside. Darkness falls.

Cindy comes outside, shining a torch.

Cindy: Furballs! Furballs!

Max: Hello? Who's there?

Cindy: Oh, hi. I didn't realise anyone was out here. I'm Cindy, the maid.

Max: Who's "Furballs"?

Cindy: That's – that's what I call the mice. The spinifex hopping mice. They come out after dark, when it's cooler. There's one over there! They're so deadly.

Max: Do you mean deadly **amazing** or deadly **lethal**?

Cindy: *(laughing)* They're deadly **amazing**! They live below ground to escape the heat of the day, and they can survive for ages without water. I'd hate for anything to happen to them.

Max: What do you think's going to happen to them?

Cindy: Er, nothing. I – I've got to go.

Cindy leaves. Max rubs his chin thoughtfully and follows.

Act 2: A Deadly Conclusion

The next morning, Max has assembled his suspects on the verandah of the eco-hotel.

Nancy: Max, why is everyone here?

Max: Because you all have a motive for stealing the frogs!

Cindy: What?

Big Bux: Outrageous!

Jimmy: Ridiculous!

Violet: As if I would do anything like that!

Nancy: Max, these people are my friends.

Max: People do strange things when they're desperate. Even you, Nancy Green!

Nancy: Why are you looking at me?

Max: Maybe you cooked up this mystery hoping the story would bring customers to your hotel.

Nancy: That's not true!

Max: People will do anything to get their name in lights. Isn't that right, Violet Highnote?

Violet: Why are you looking at me?

Max: Maybe you got rid of the frogs so Nancy would hire you to sing.

Violet: I wouldn't do that!

Max: No? Some people go to crazy lengths for a job, don't they, Jimmy Presto?

Jimmy: Why are you looking at me?

Max: Maybe you got rid of the frogs so you could get your big break with a news story!

Jimmy: I wouldn't hurt a fly!

Max: Ah, but there is someone who **would** hurt a fly, isn't there, Cindy? Someone called – Furballs!

Cindy: Why are you looking at me?

Max: Furballs isn't a name for the mice, is it Cindy? Furballs ... is a cat!

Max pulls the cat from his trench coat pocket.

Max: Say hello, Furballs.

Furballs nuzzles Max's face.

Cindy takes Furballs from Max.

Cindy: Thank goodness you found him, Max!

Nancy: Cindy! Pets are not allowed here!

Cindy: I know, but I needed this job and I couldn't find a new home for him. He escaped from my room.

Nancy: You know he can't stay here, Cindy. During the day it's much too hot in the desert, and at night cats become hunters.

Cindy: I'm sorry, Nancy. I will find him a new home.

Nancy: Max – did Furballs kill my singing frogs?

Max: Kid, there's no such thing as a singing frog.

Big Bux: I told you so! She made them up!

Max: Did she? Maybe there's another explanation – Big Bux McGee!

Big Bux: Why are you looking at me?

Max: I did a little digging down at the claypan. Do you know what I found? Frogs – dozens of them!

Nancy gasps in surprise.

Nancy: What are you talking about?

Max: Tell her the truth this time, Big Bux!

Big Bux: You want the truth? The truth is that Nancy knows nothing about the desert. She couldn't identify a trilling frog if her life depended on it!

Nancy: **Trilling** frog?

Big Bux: That's right. They're trilling frogs. When it rains, there's hundreds of them, but when the water dries up, they bury themselves under the ground.

Nancy: For how long?

Big Bux: You might not see your precious frogs again for months – even years! They'll stay underground until it rains again.

Nancy: Why didn't you tell me?

Big Bux: I wanted you to give up and leave, so I could buy your eco-hotel at a bargain price!

Nancy: I see. Well, nice try, Big Bux, but I'm not going anywhere!

Big Bux: We'll see about that! No one's going to come to your eco-hotel now!

Nancy: (*sighing*) You may be mean, but you're right. No one will come now that the trilling frogs have gone underground. What if they stay down there for years? What am I going to do?

Jimmy's phone beeps. He checks the message.

Jimmy: I wouldn't worry, Nancy. This hotel is about to be swamped with bookings!

Violet: Finally, I'll have a proper audience!

Nancy: What? Why?

Jimmy: I wrote an article about Violet. It'll be published in tomorrow's paper. People will soon be flying in from all over Australia to hear the hotel's Fabulous Froggy!

Violet: Oh Jimmy! This is a dream come true!

Max: And Big Bux is wrong, Nancy. You're as tough as a thorny devil and you love this place. I think you **do** belong out here.

Nancy: Thank you, Max. Thank you for everything. And as for **you**, Big Bux, you're going to make this up to me. You're going to teach me everything you know about the desert. Deal?

Big Bux: You **are** as tough as a thorny devil! Deal.

Max: It looks like a happy ending all round. That's my cue to leave.

Nancy: Don't go, Max!

Max: A man like me is better off alone.

Cindy: Ow, Furballs, don't scratch me!

Violet: Max, wait. Why don't you adopt Furballs?

Max: What?

Cindy: Yes, he likes you more than he likes me!

Max: I don't have time for a –

Furballs jumps into Max's arms.

Max: Awww! Look at his wittle face!

Max gets ready to leave.

Max: All right, Furballs. I'll show you the city. I think you'll like it. There are shadows, alleyways and rats. The city is just the place for cool cats like you and me.

Nancy: You won't be alone after all. Take care, Max.

Max: You too, kid. I'll never forget this place. It's been ... deadly.